EXPLORING
Stella's Island

Bonilou Stella Custer

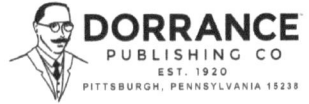

The contents of this work, including, but not limited to, the accuracy of events, people, and places depicted; opinions expressed; permission to use previously published materials included; and any advice given or actions advocated are solely the responsibility of the author, who assumes all liability for said work and indemnifies the publisher against any claims stemming from publication of the work.

All Rights Reserved
Copyright © 2022 by Bonilou Stella Custer

No part of this book may be reproduced or transmitted, downloaded, distributed, reverse engineered, or stored in or introduced into any information storage and retrieval system, in any form or by any means, including photocopying and recording, whether electronic or mechanical, now known or hereinafter invented without permission in writing from the publisher.

Dorrance Publishing Co
585 Alpha Drive
Suite 103
Pittsburgh, PA 15238
Visit our website at *www.dorrancebookstore.com*

ISBN: 978-1-6853-7364-1
eISBN: 978-1-6853-7678-9

This book is dedicated to Jamie Hoag and our grandchildren.

A special thank-you to:

Jackquline McCann

Melda Turcotte

Bobbijo Decker

John Custer

Barbara Villegas

Sandra Harper

Cassandra Decker

Dust To Diamonds, S.A., Tx

8 bunnies, 5 butterflies, 5 cats, 1 bird, 6 baby dolls, 2 sunglasses, 1 gnome, 4 turtles, 1 squirrel, 4 dogs, 3 leprechauns, 3 mushrooms, 3 lambs, 36 rainbows, 1 alligator, girl's name, 5 plotted plants, 1 fairy, 1 unicorn, 1 hut

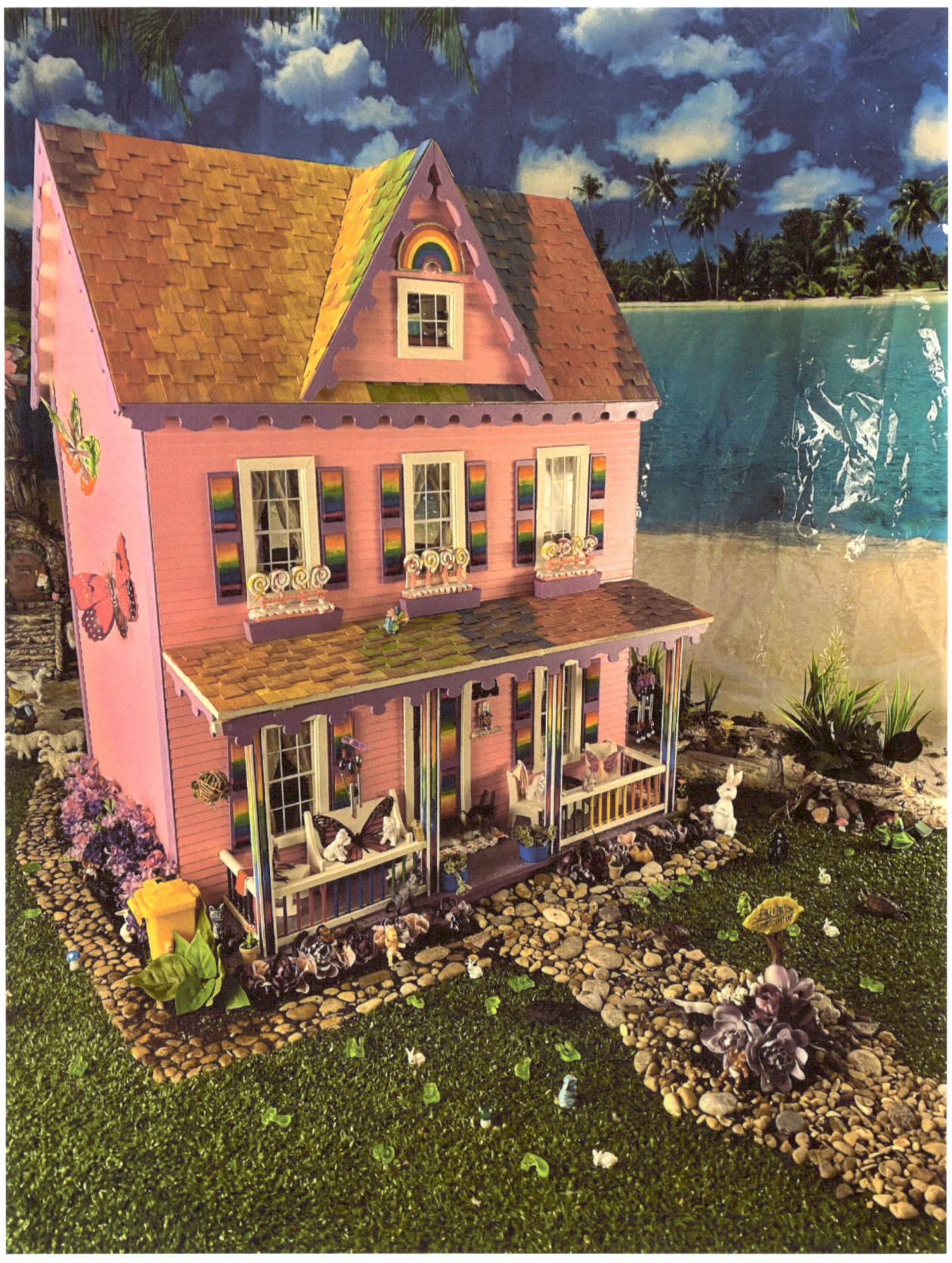

How many differences can you find from page 1?

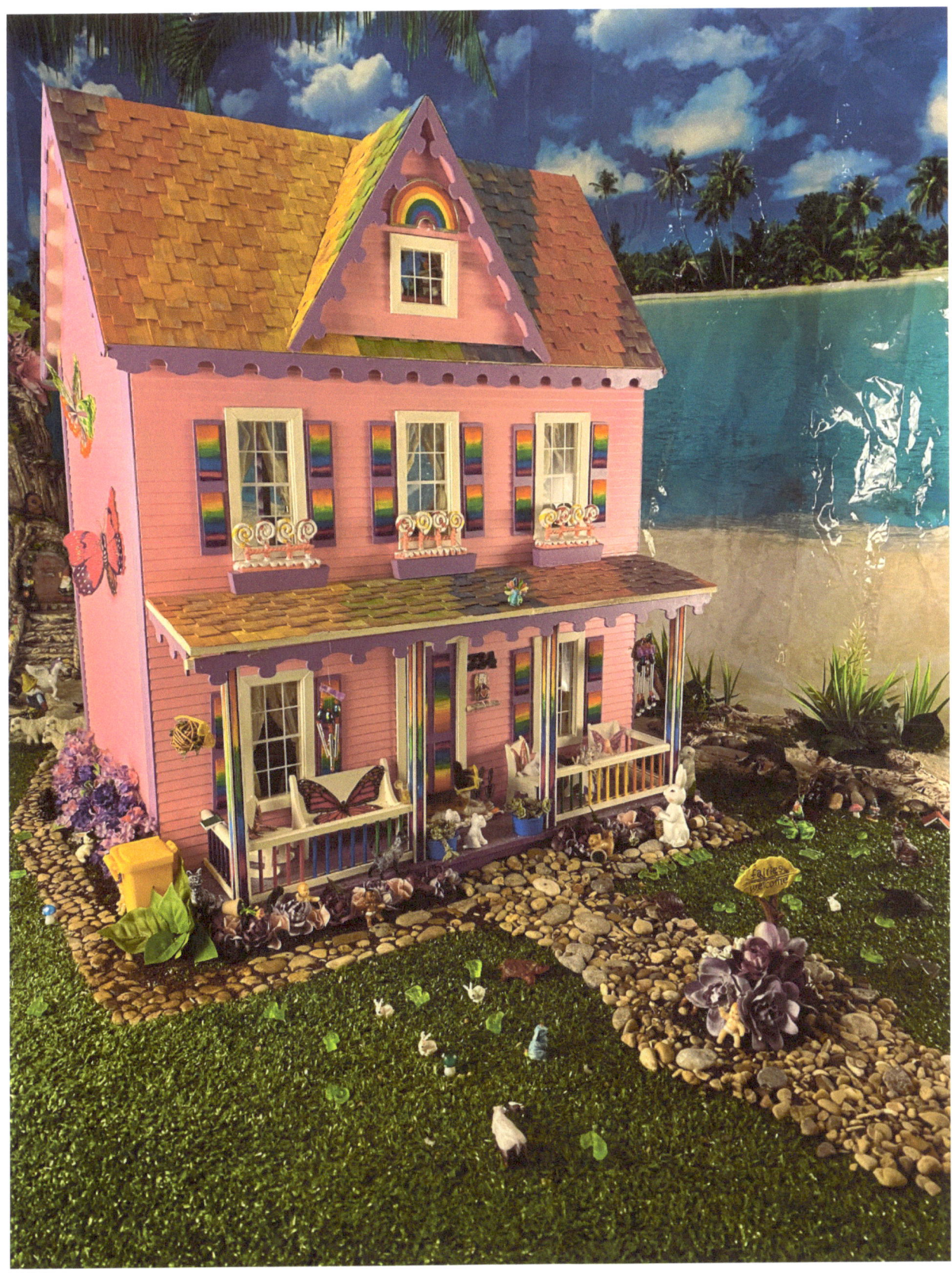

7 bunnies, 1 crashed fairy, 1 turtle, 2 fairies, 7 mushrooms, 3 pumpkins, 3 cats, 1 squirrel, boy's name, 1 walrus, 1 frog, 1 koala bear, 7 gnomes, 2 books, 2 butterflies

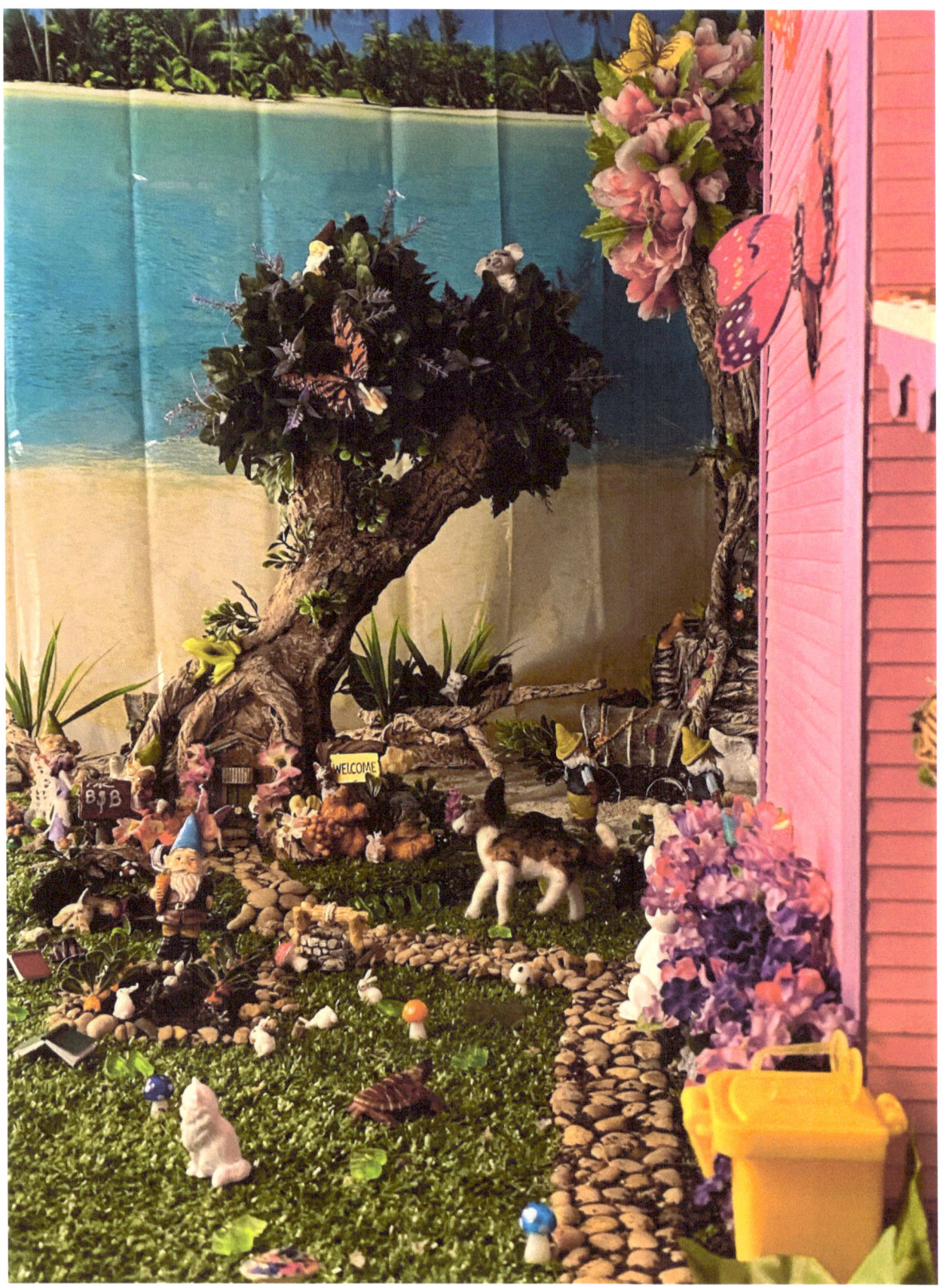

4 gnomes, 4 bunnies, 3 dogs, 3 unicorns, 3 wagons, 7 baby dolls, 3 lambs, 3 fairies, 4 turtle, 7 doors, 1 bear cave, 1 cat, 1 mushroom, 1 hut, 1 frog, 6 tables

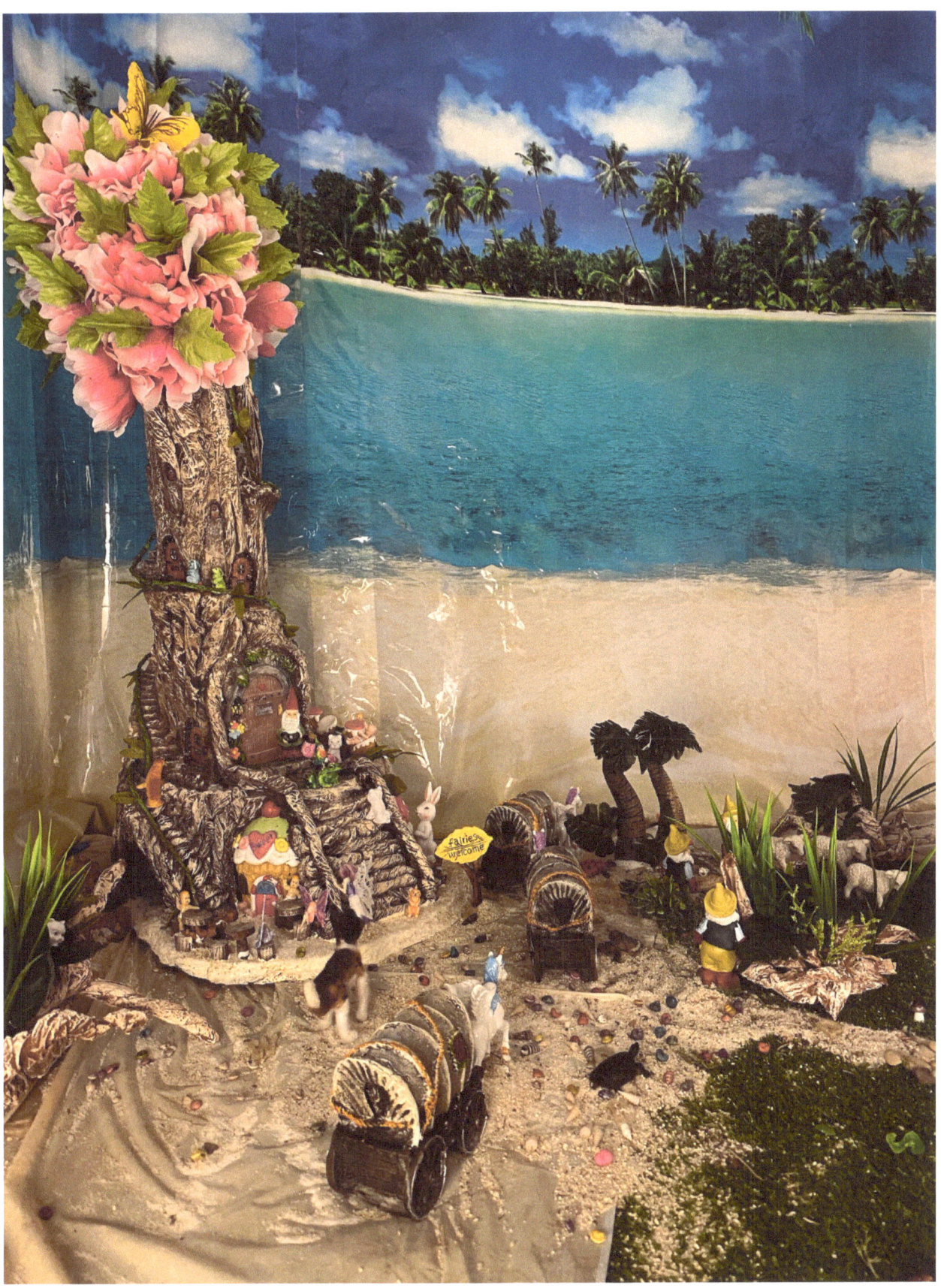

6 baby dolls, 4 gnomes, 2 fairies, 2 purple unicorns, 5 orange shells, 4 turtles, 3 signs, 1 honey badger, 7 blue shells, 1 lamb, 1 leprechaun, 6 bunnies, 3 wagons, 7 red shells, 1 cherry

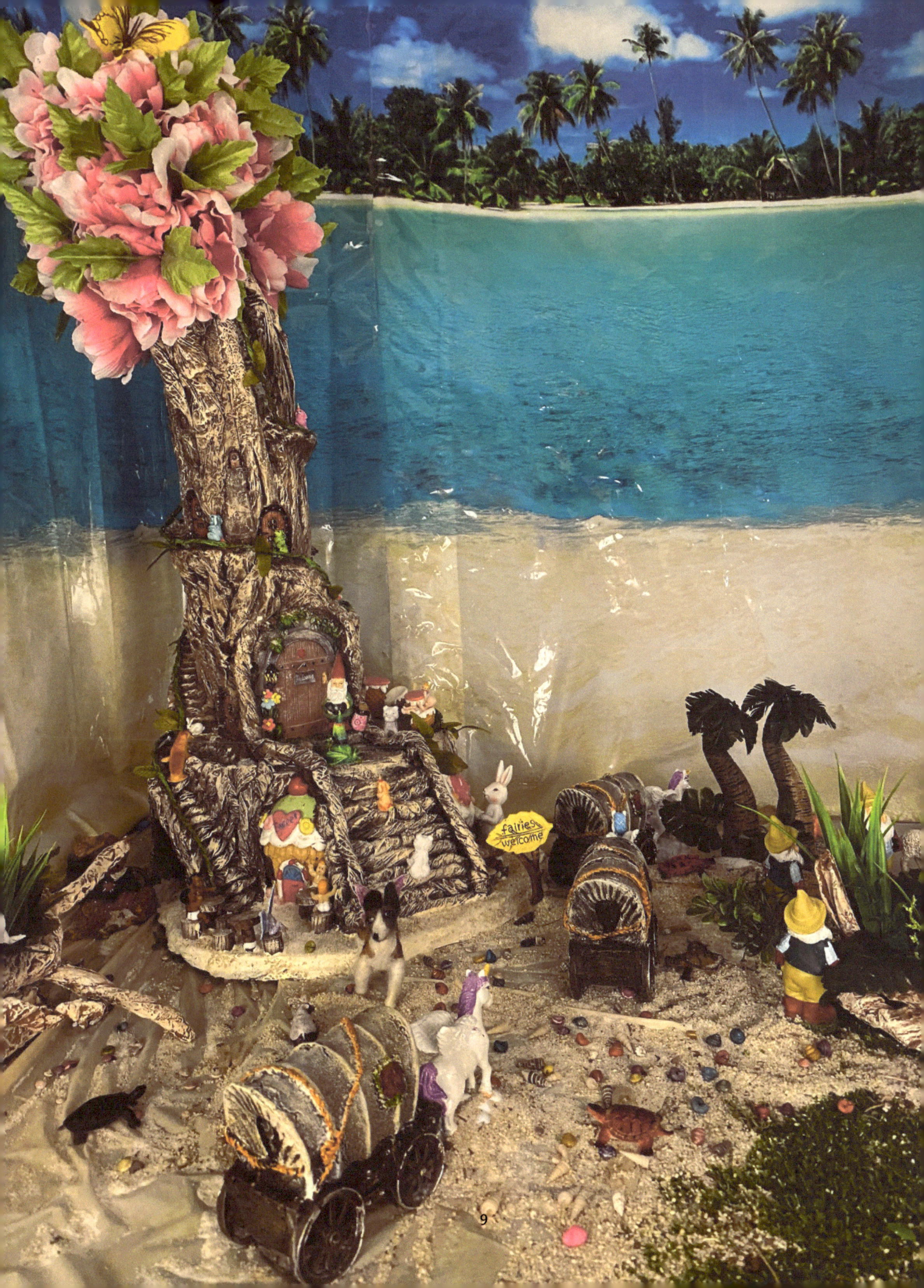

2 books, 6 baby dolls, 8 bunnies, 1 doughnut, 1 walrus, 4 cats, 2 honey badgers, 2 wagons, 1 skunk, 7 gnomes, 9 mushrooms, 5 turtles, 1 bear, 4 dogs, 1 frog

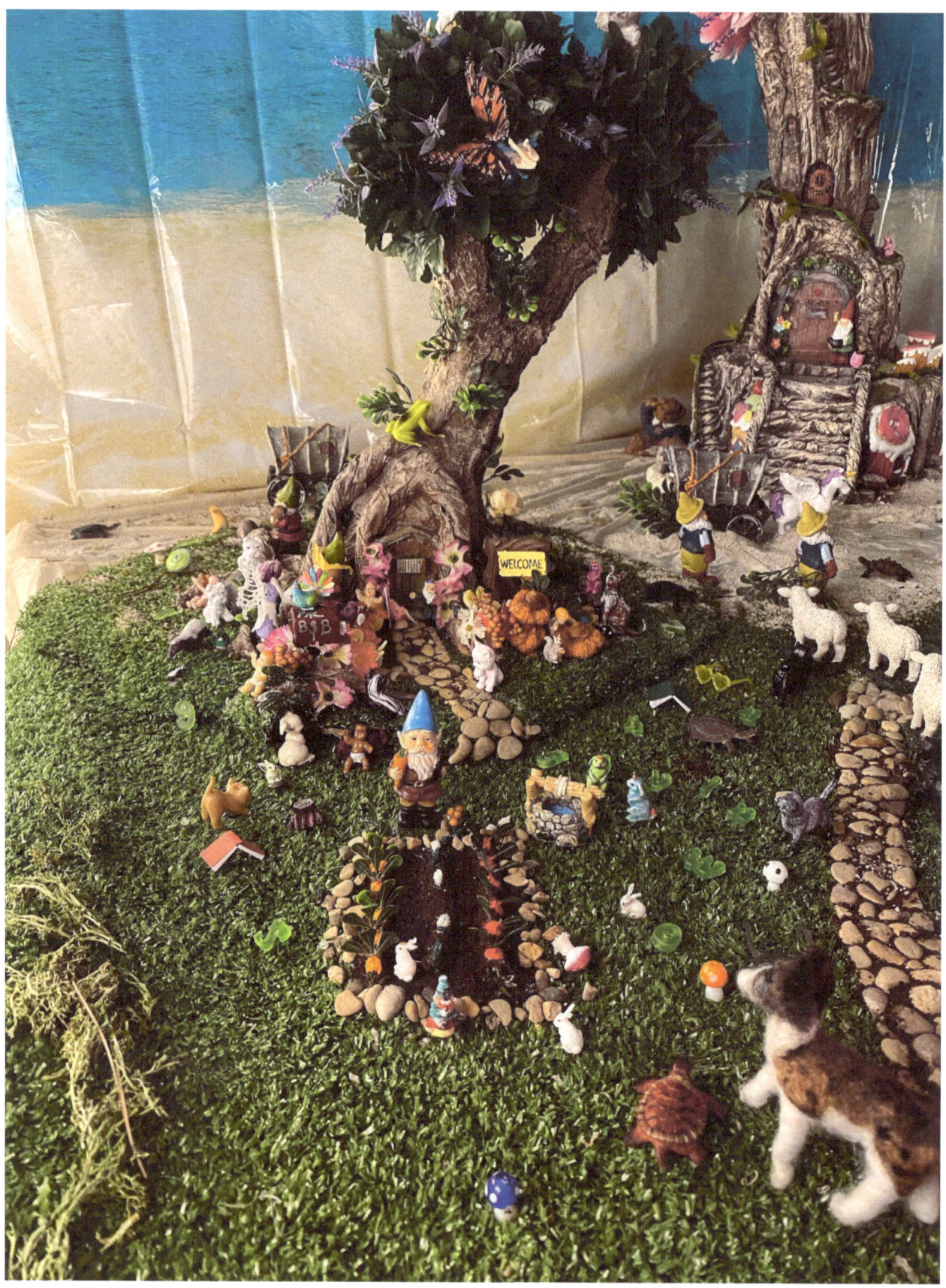

How many differences can you find from page 6?

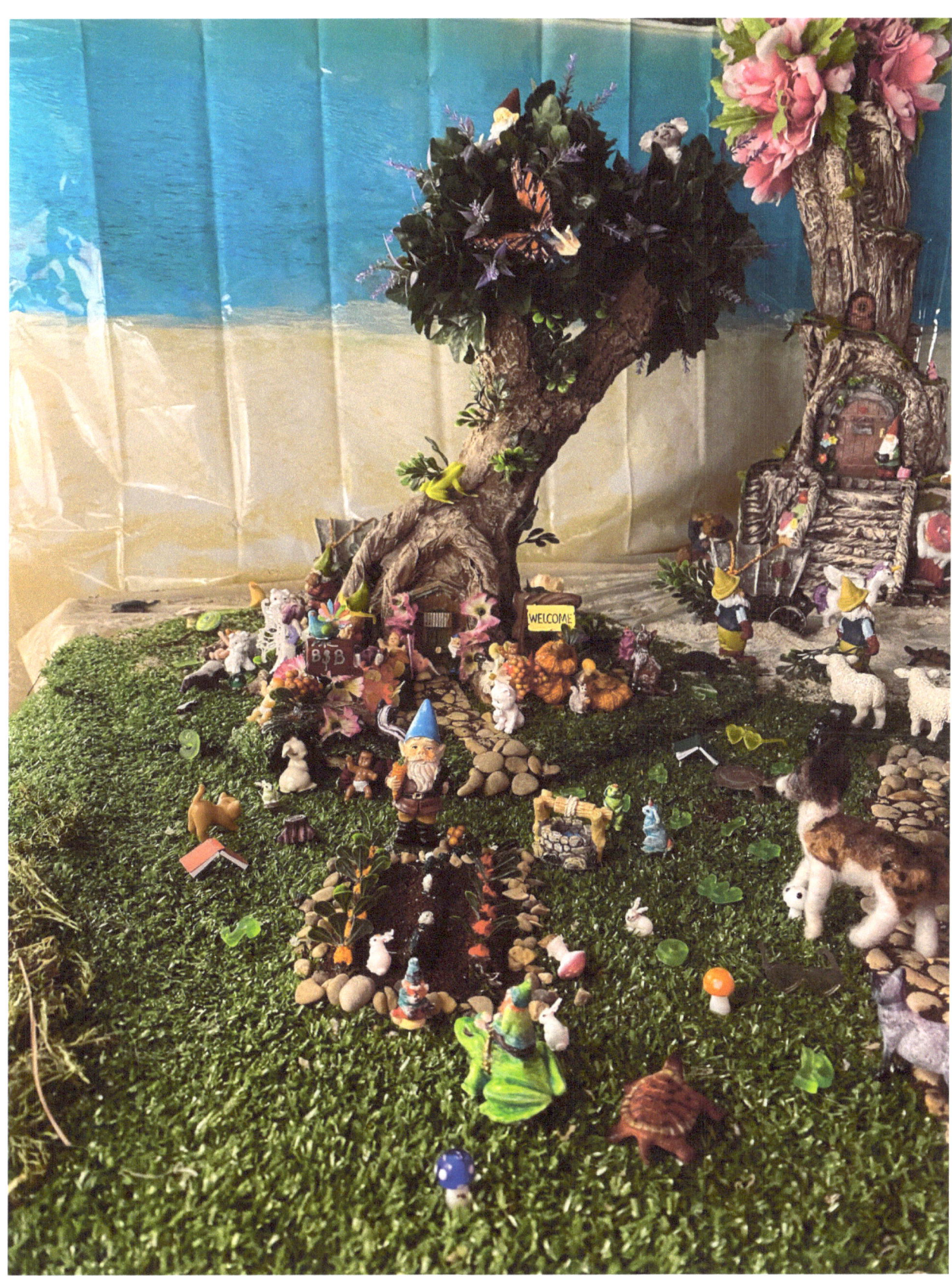

How many differences can you find from page 9?

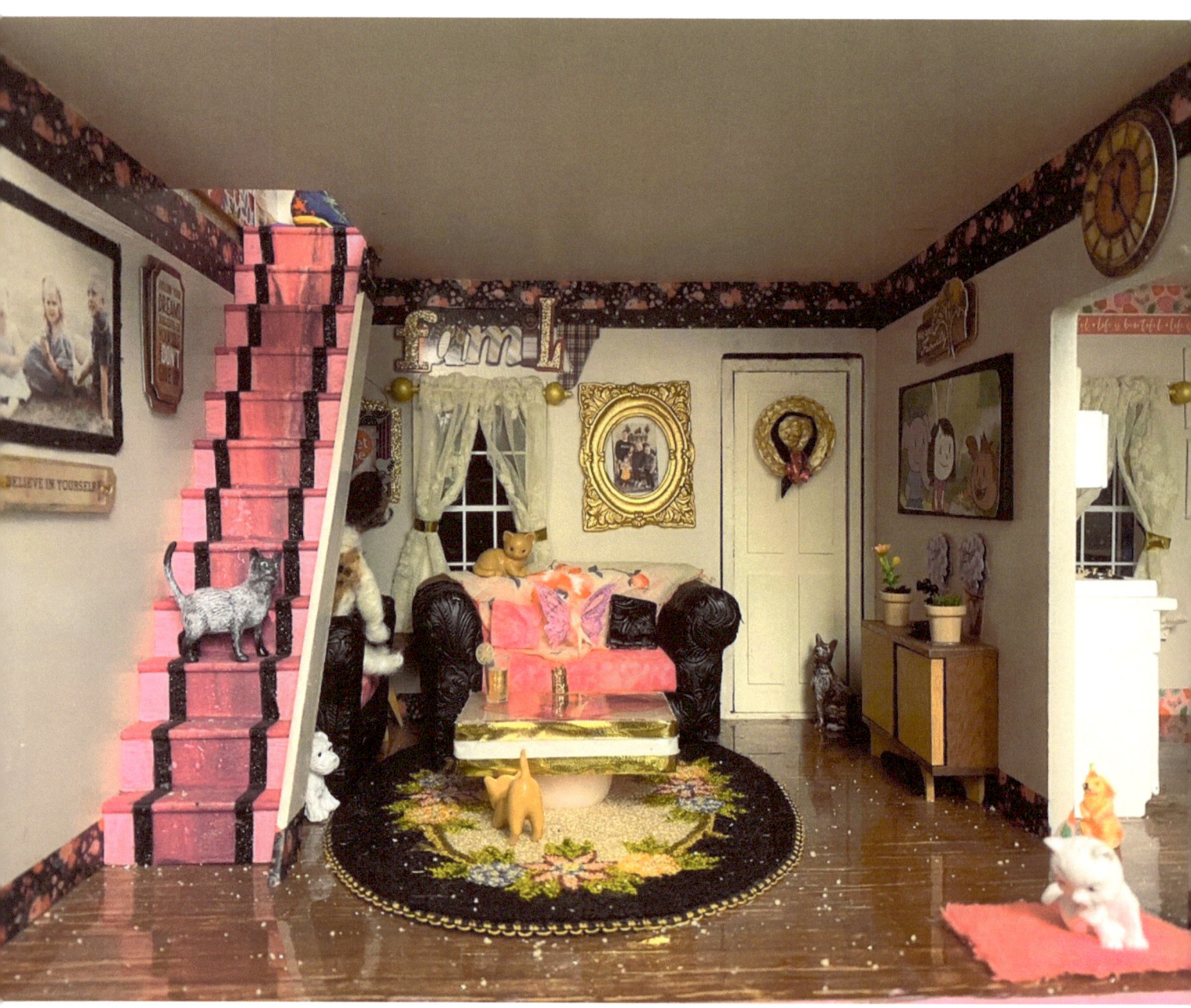

5 potted plants, 1 rolling pin, 5 cats, 1 bunny, 1 phone, 1 dog, 1 tree, 1 hat, a dream, 2 family (the word), 4 hearts, dollars, mixer, 3 balls

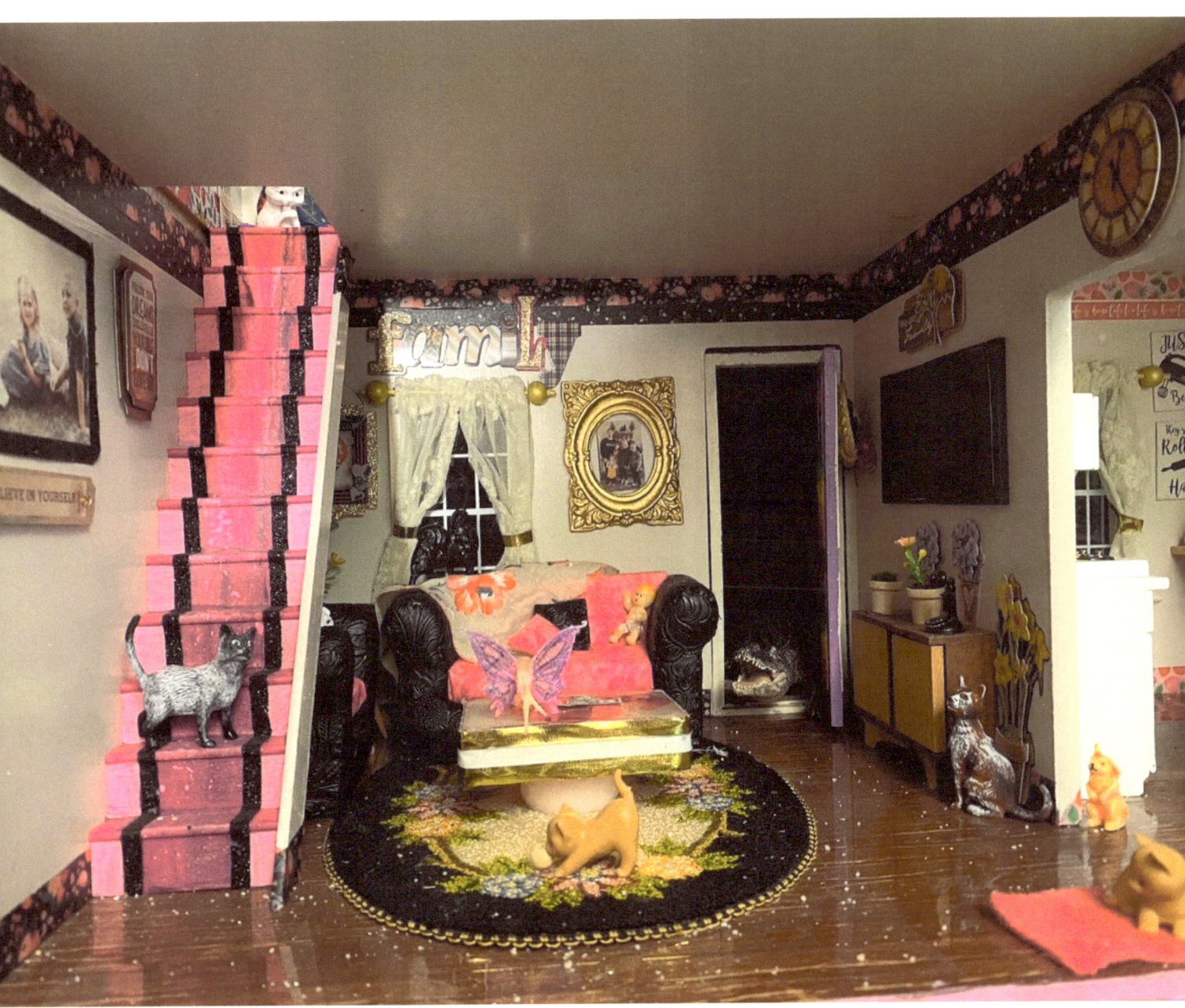

How many differences can you find from page 9?

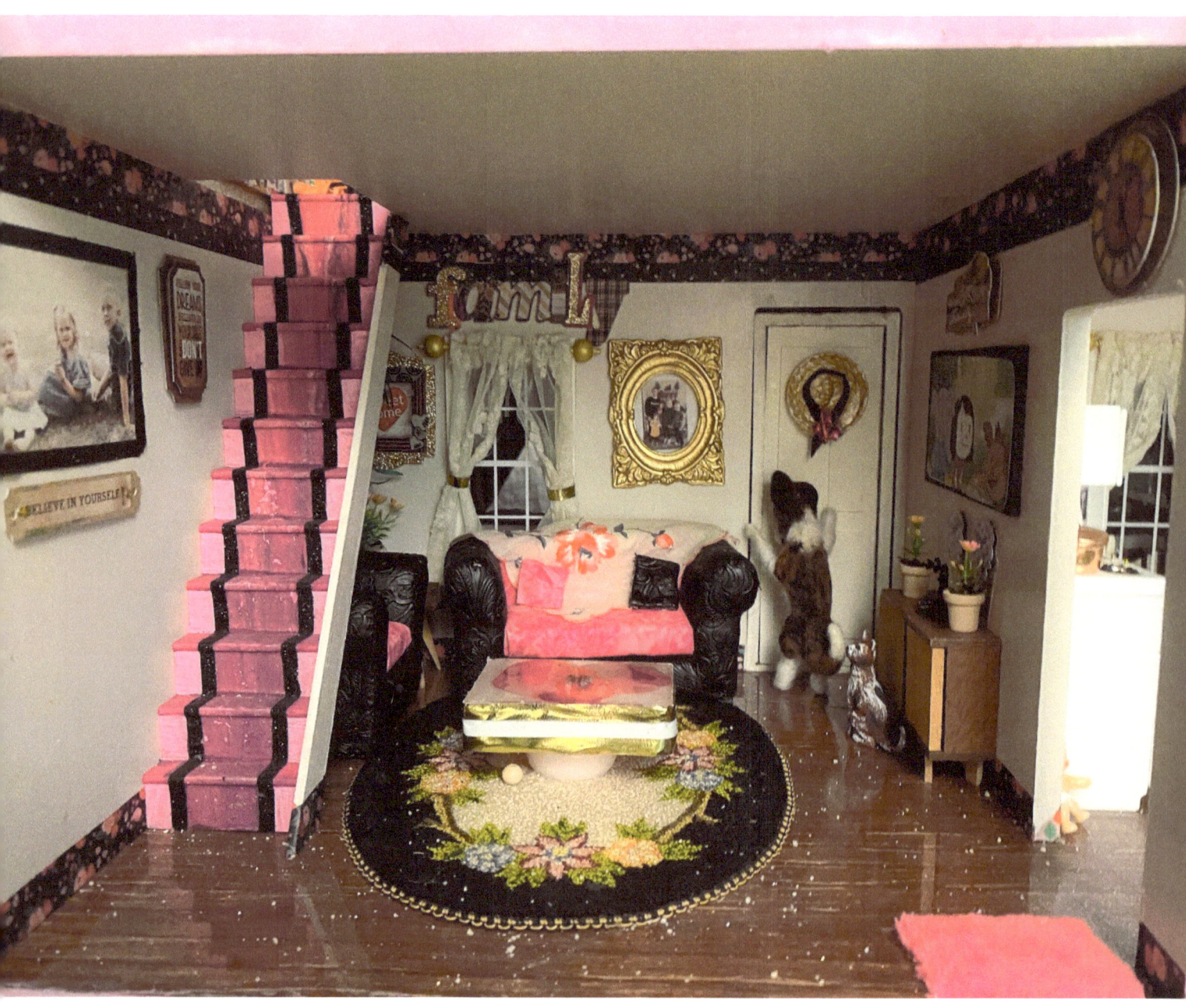

4 child's paintings, tea, 2 forks, whisk, 2 baby dolls, toes, squirrel, teapot, large strawberry, 3 cups, creatures (the word), leftovers (the word), mixer, 4 jars

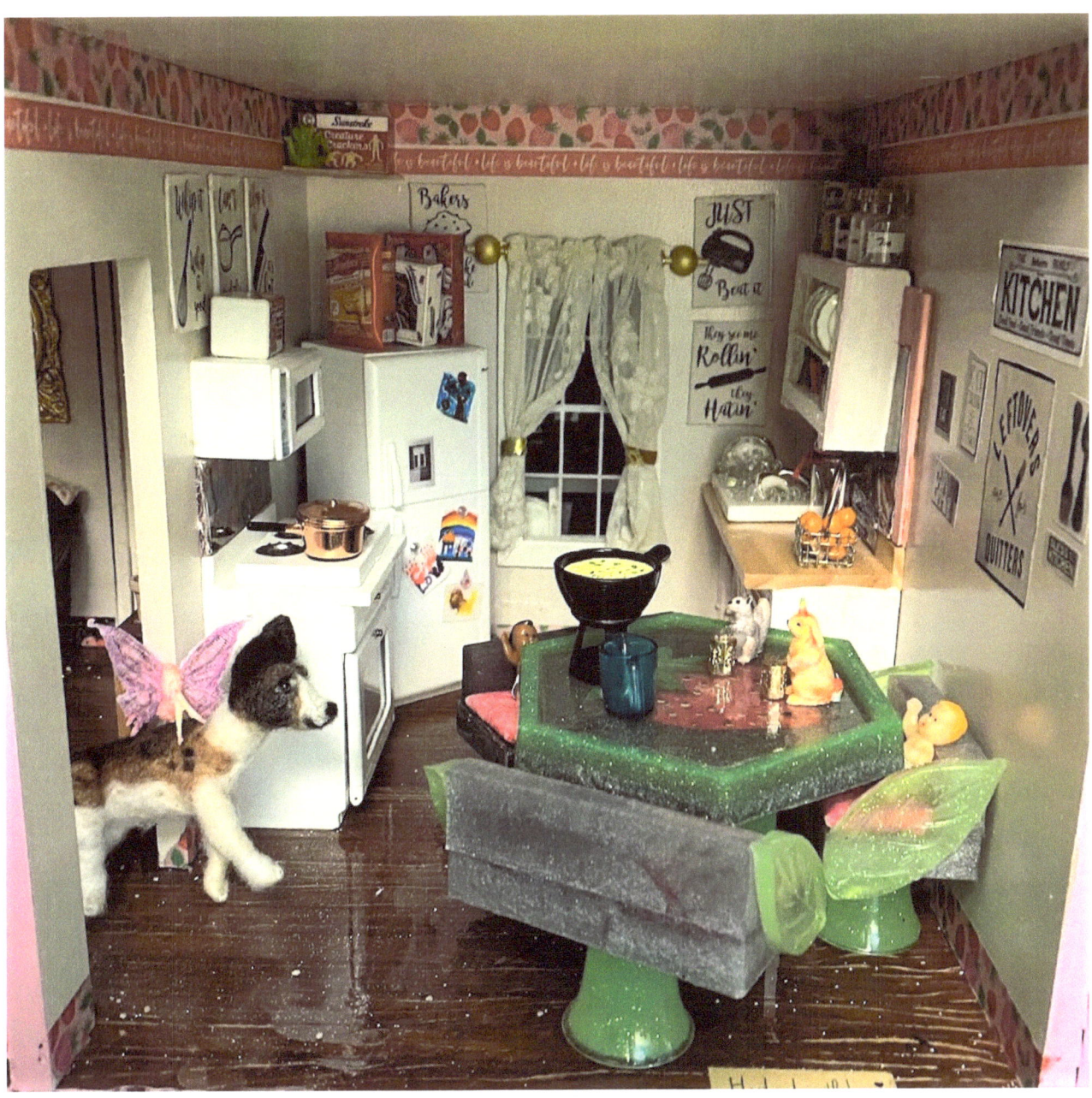

How many differences can you find from page 11?

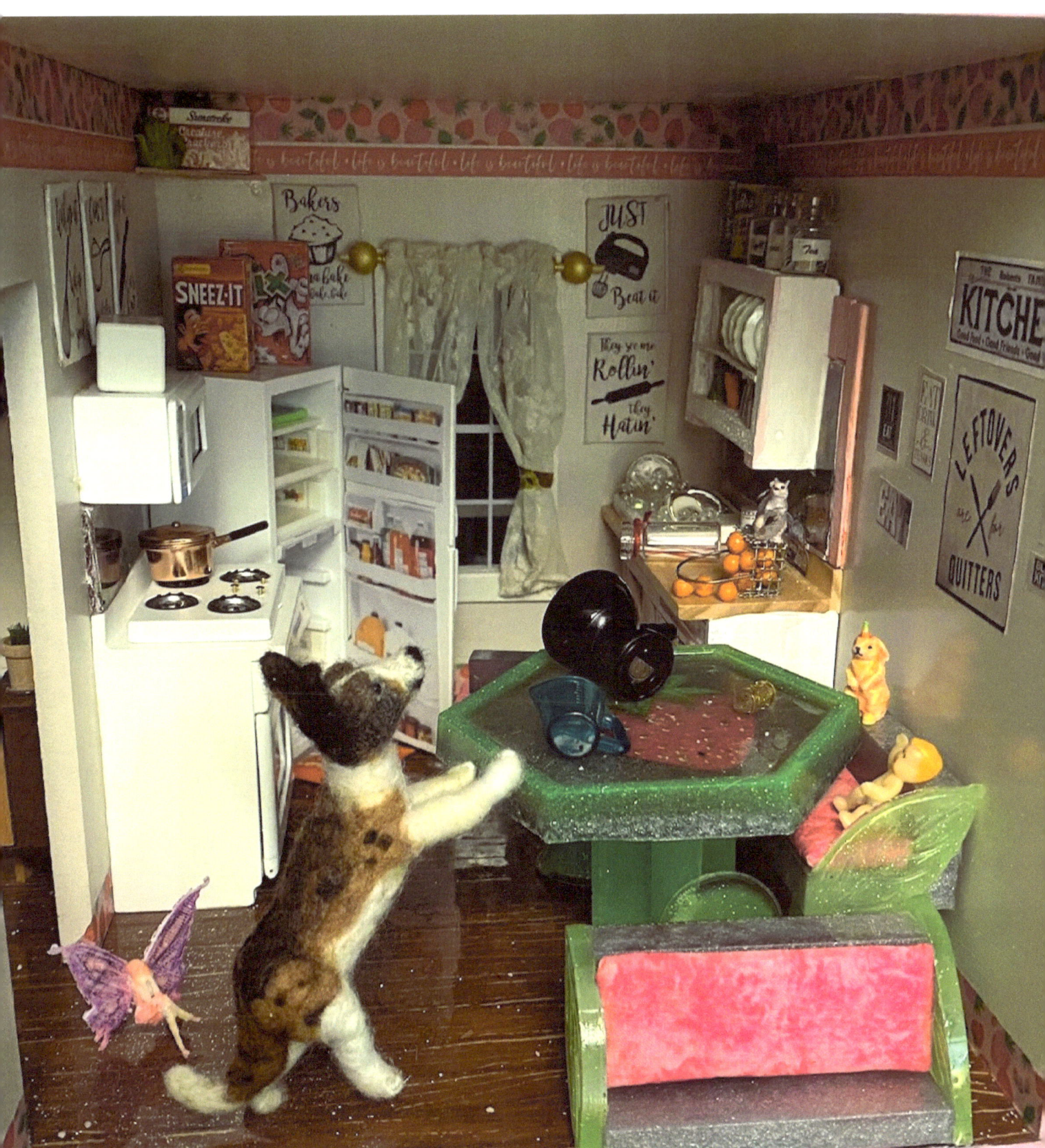

11 shoes, 8 purses, 2 baby dolls, 2 cats, 7 dogs, 2 sunglasses, 3 necklaces, 6 potted plants, 4 shells, 6 lollipops, 3 family photos, book, house, pyramid, 2 birds

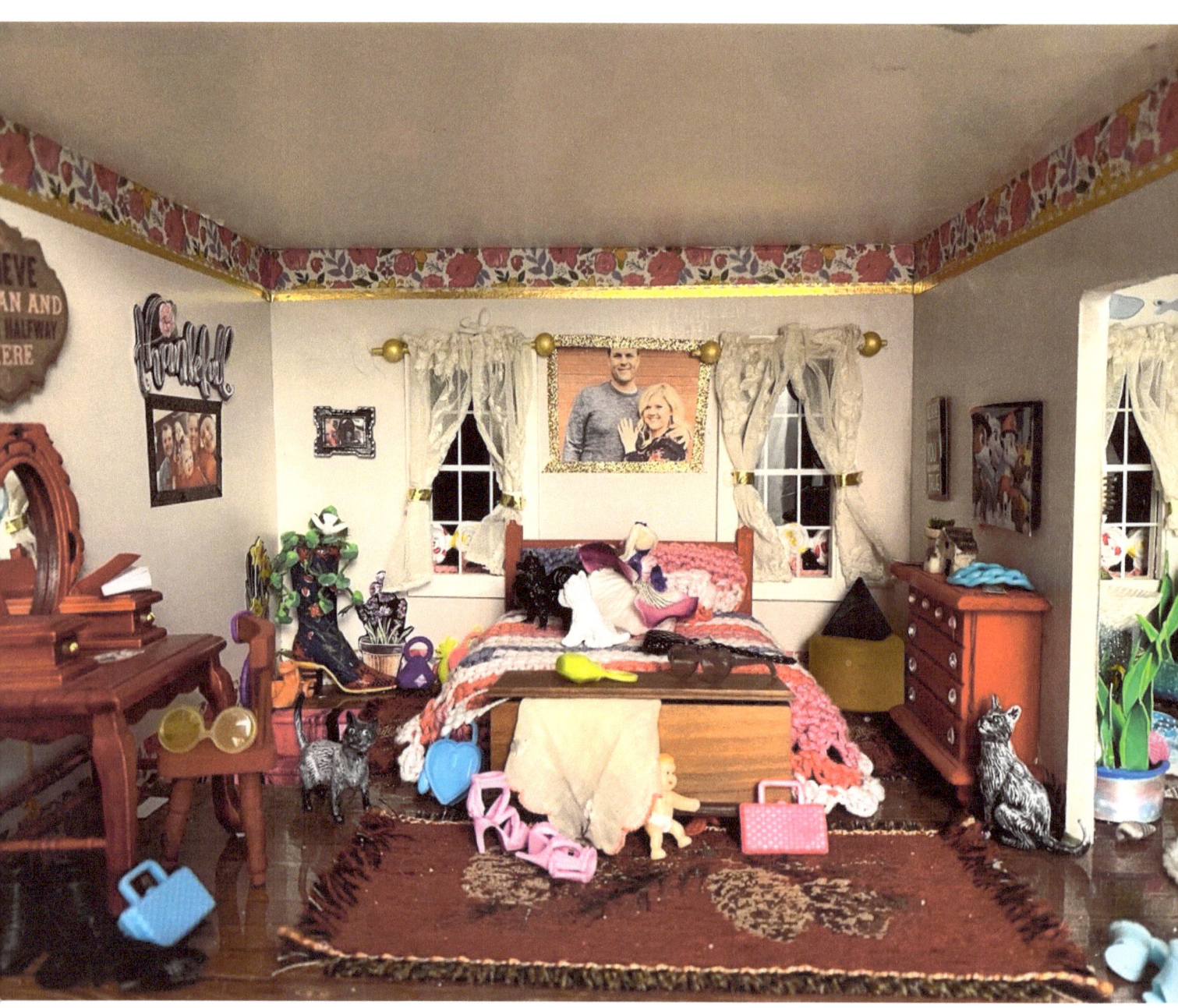

How many differences can you find from page 13?

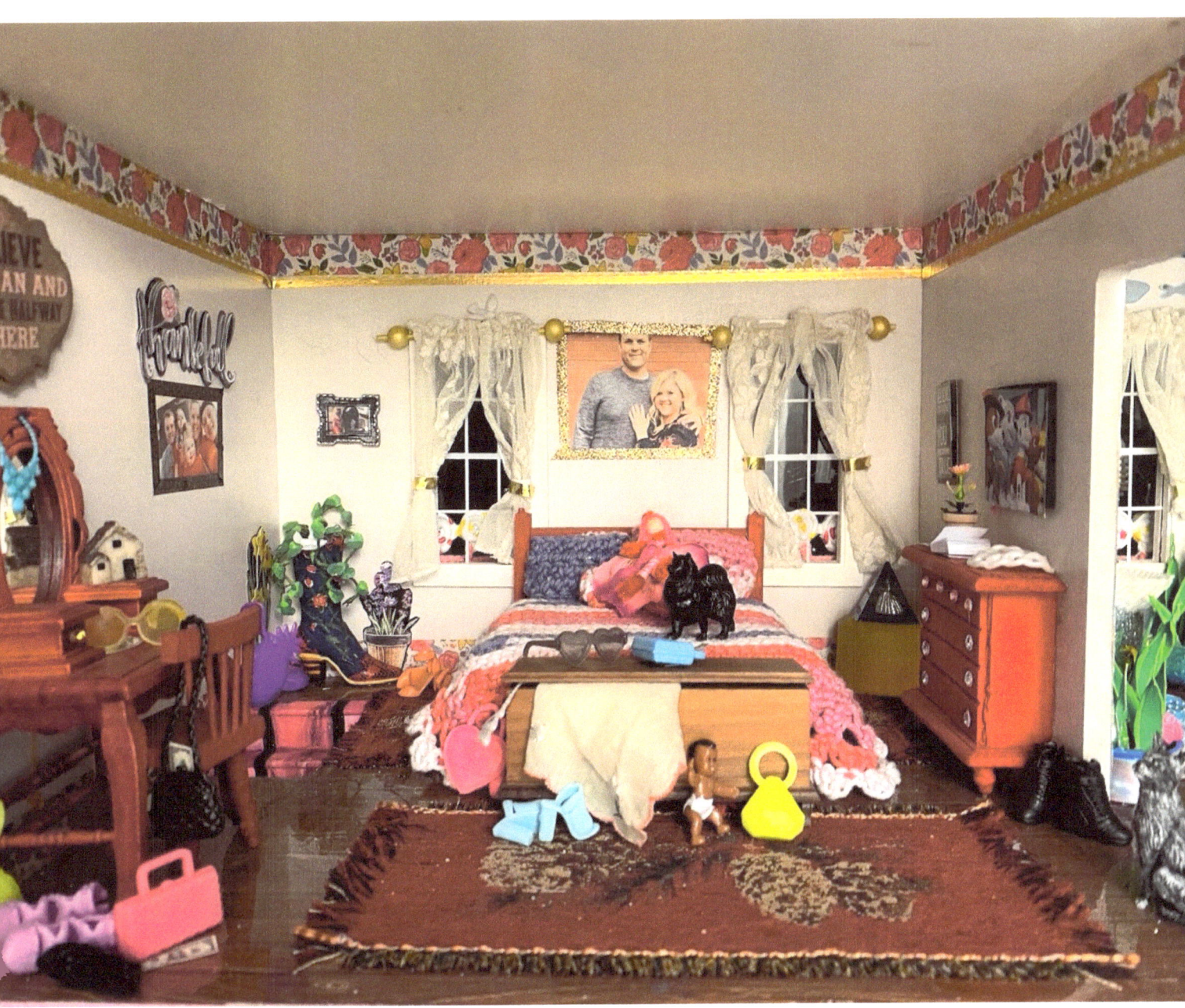

Sneer (the word), 16 fish, bird, 2 seahorses, 13 shells, fairy, turtle, 2 potted plants, 3 whales, 1 octopus, plunger, 2 rugs, toothbrush

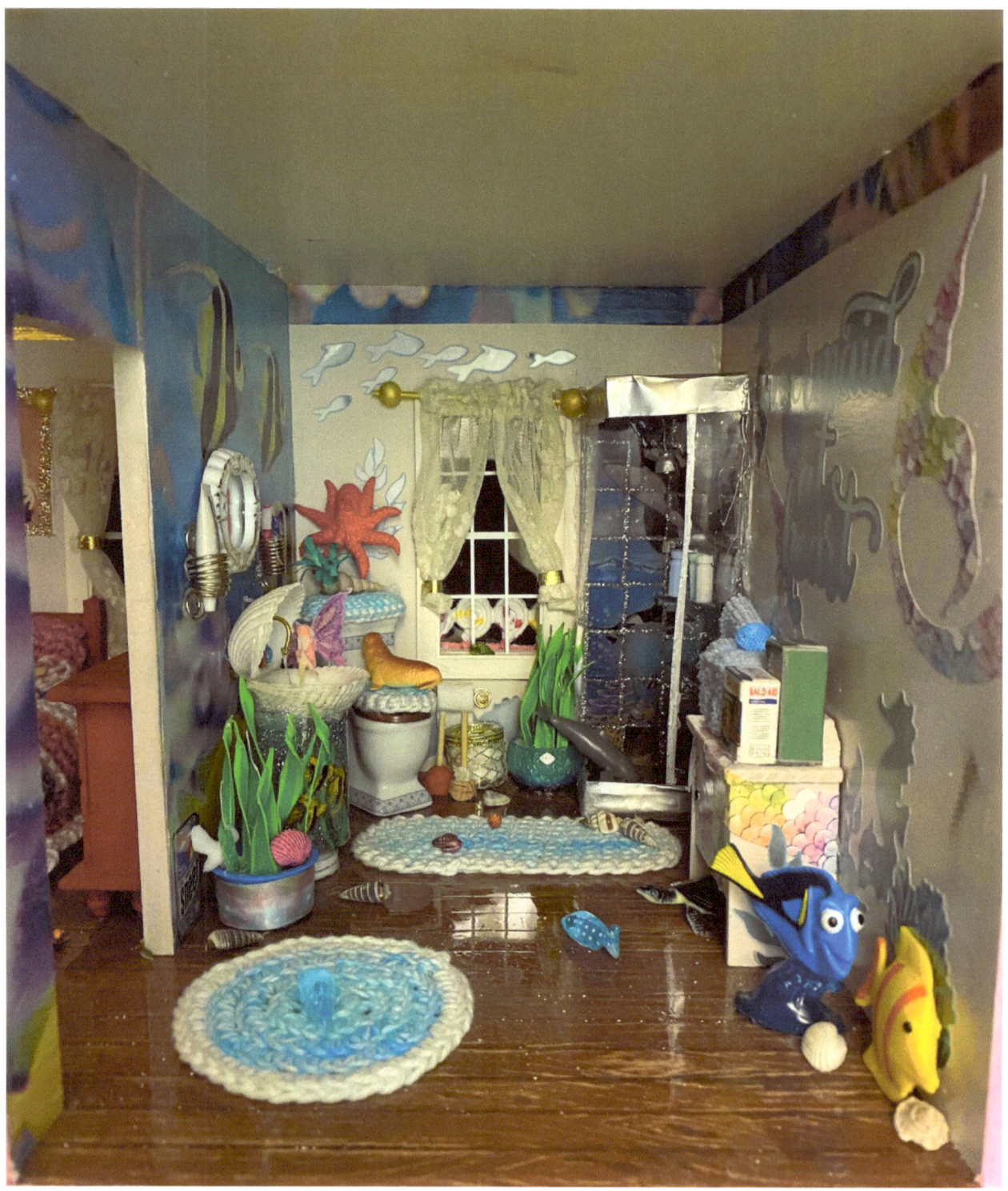

How many differences can you find from page 15?

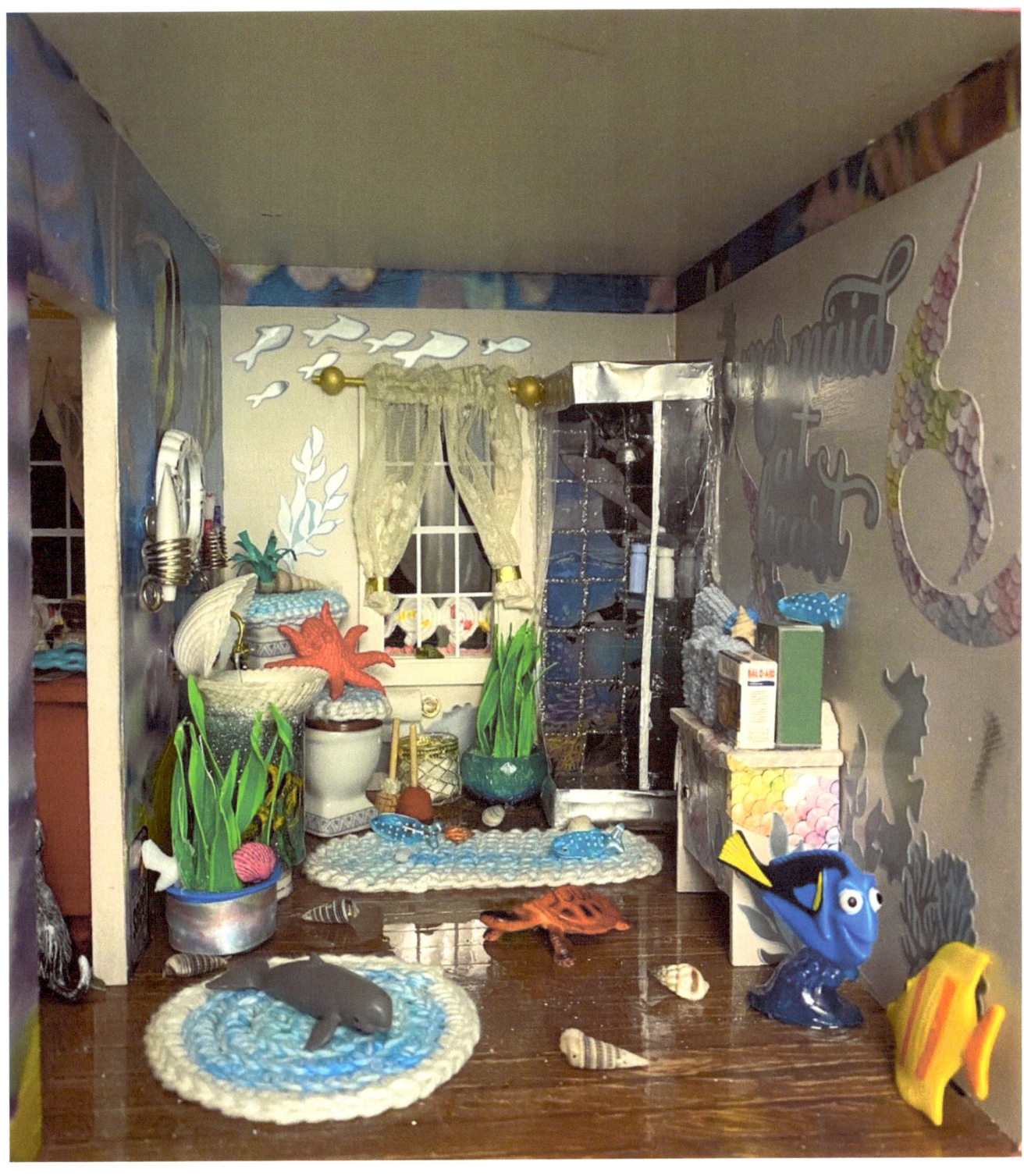

How many differences can you find from page 16?

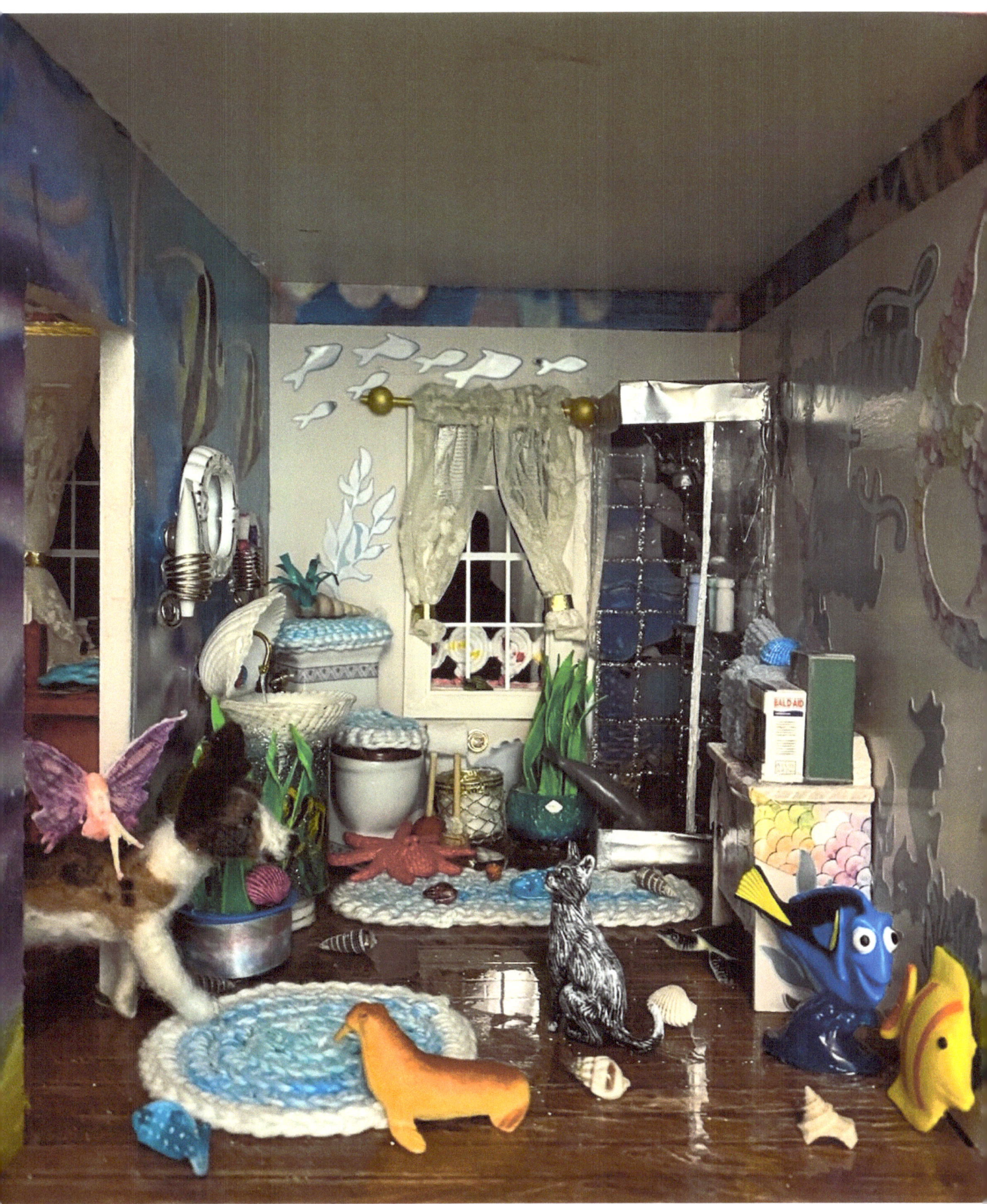

6 baby dolls, 5 bottles, 2 fairies, cat, 2 dogs, sunglasses, LOVE, shoe, high chair, flowers, 2 baby buggies, 2 cribs, BELIEVE, sheep, E, T

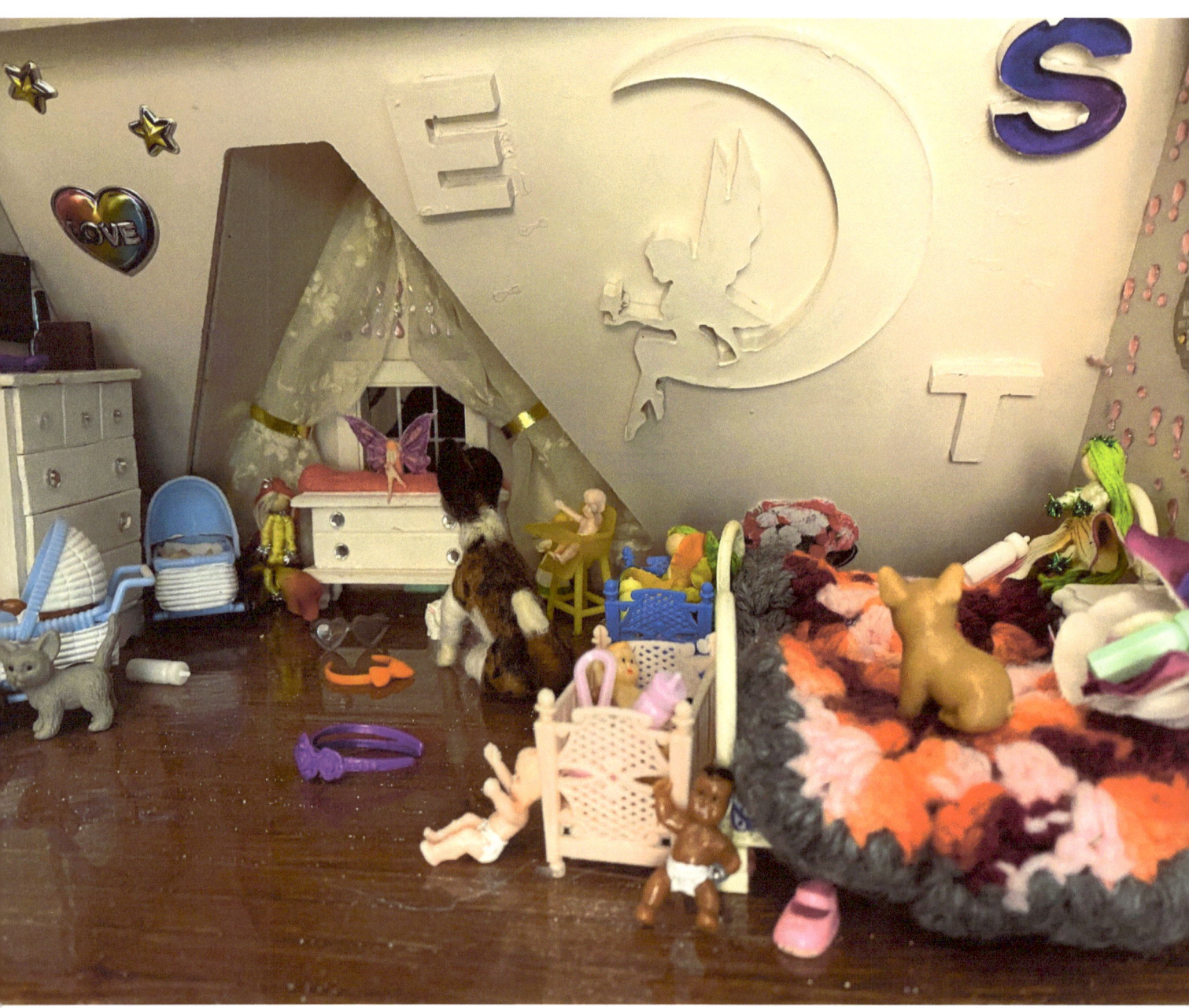

How many differences can you find from page 18?

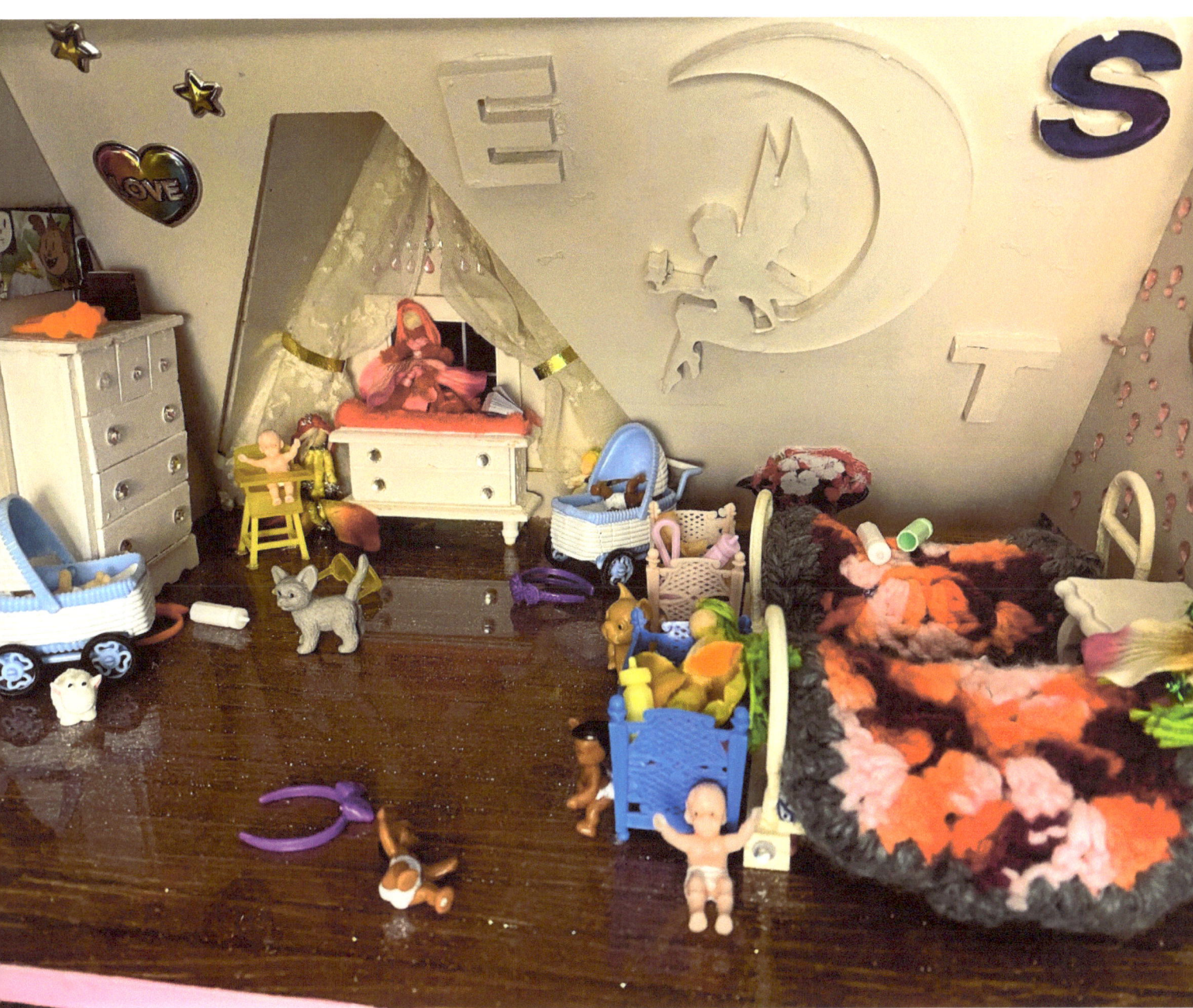

How many differences can you find from page 21?

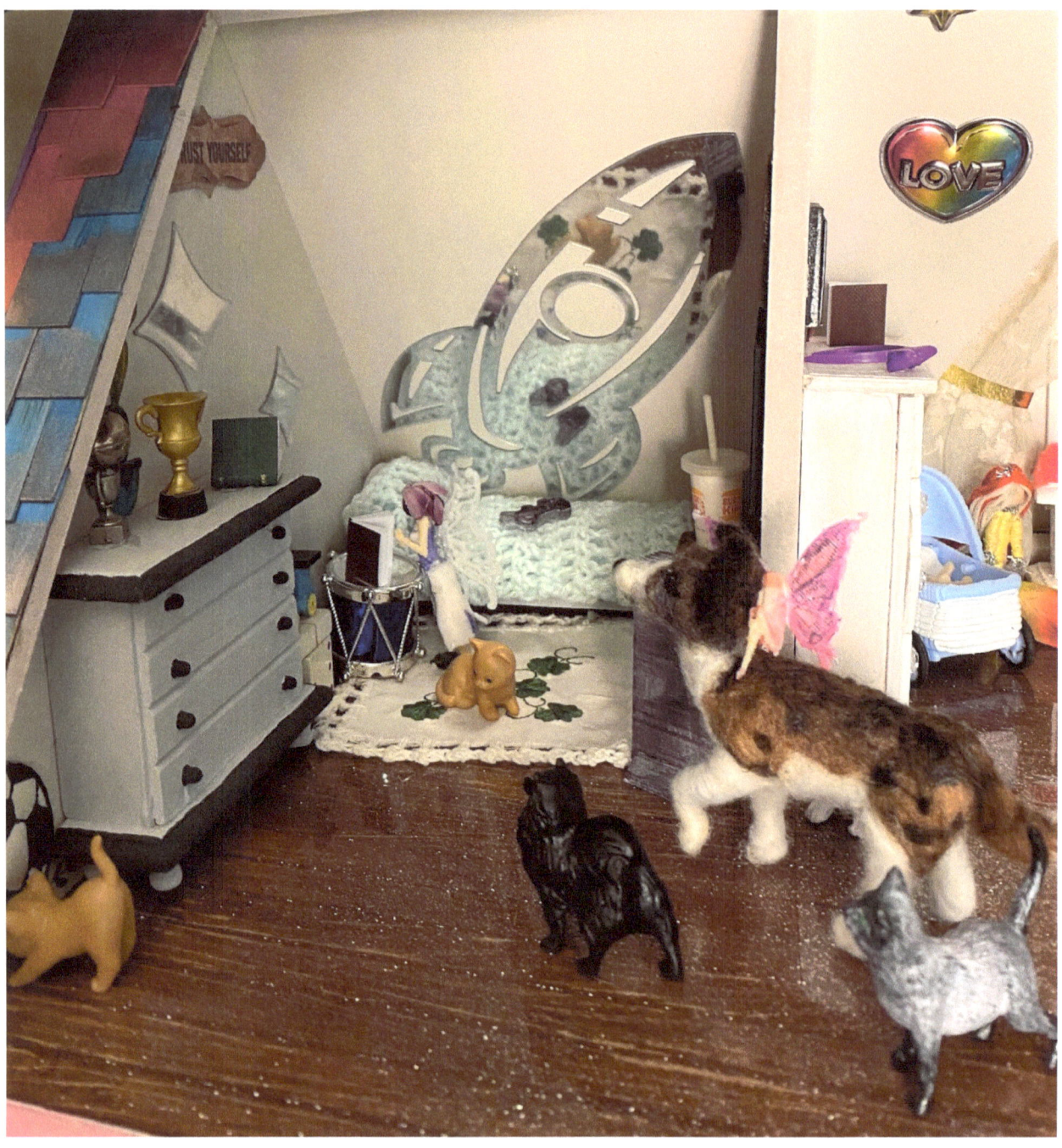

2 cats, 3 dogs, YOURSELF, 2 books, 10 clovers, 1 game controller, 2 fairies, drum, football, 3 mirrors, star, 2 trophies, baby buggy, headband

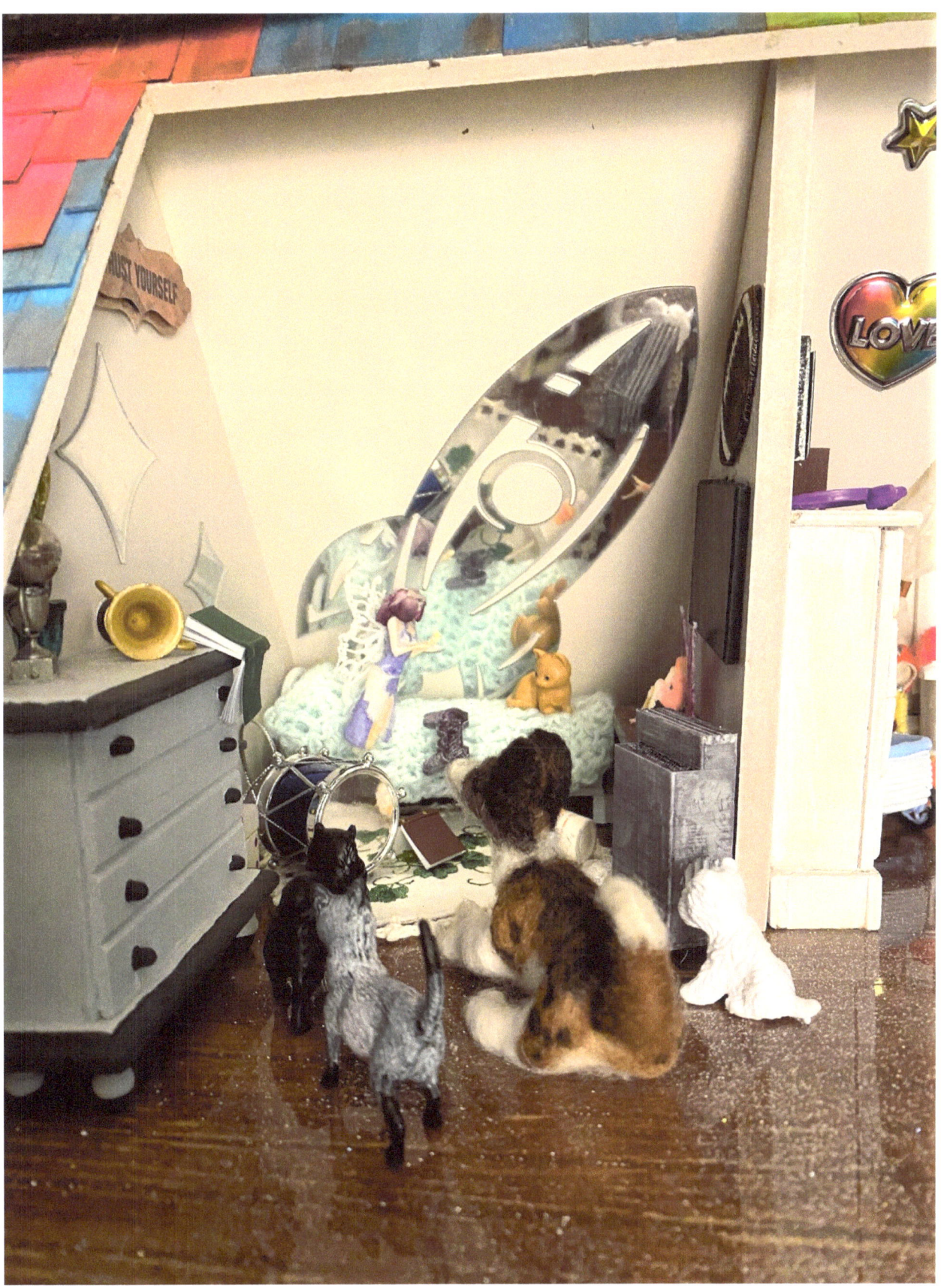

Can you find all the readable things?

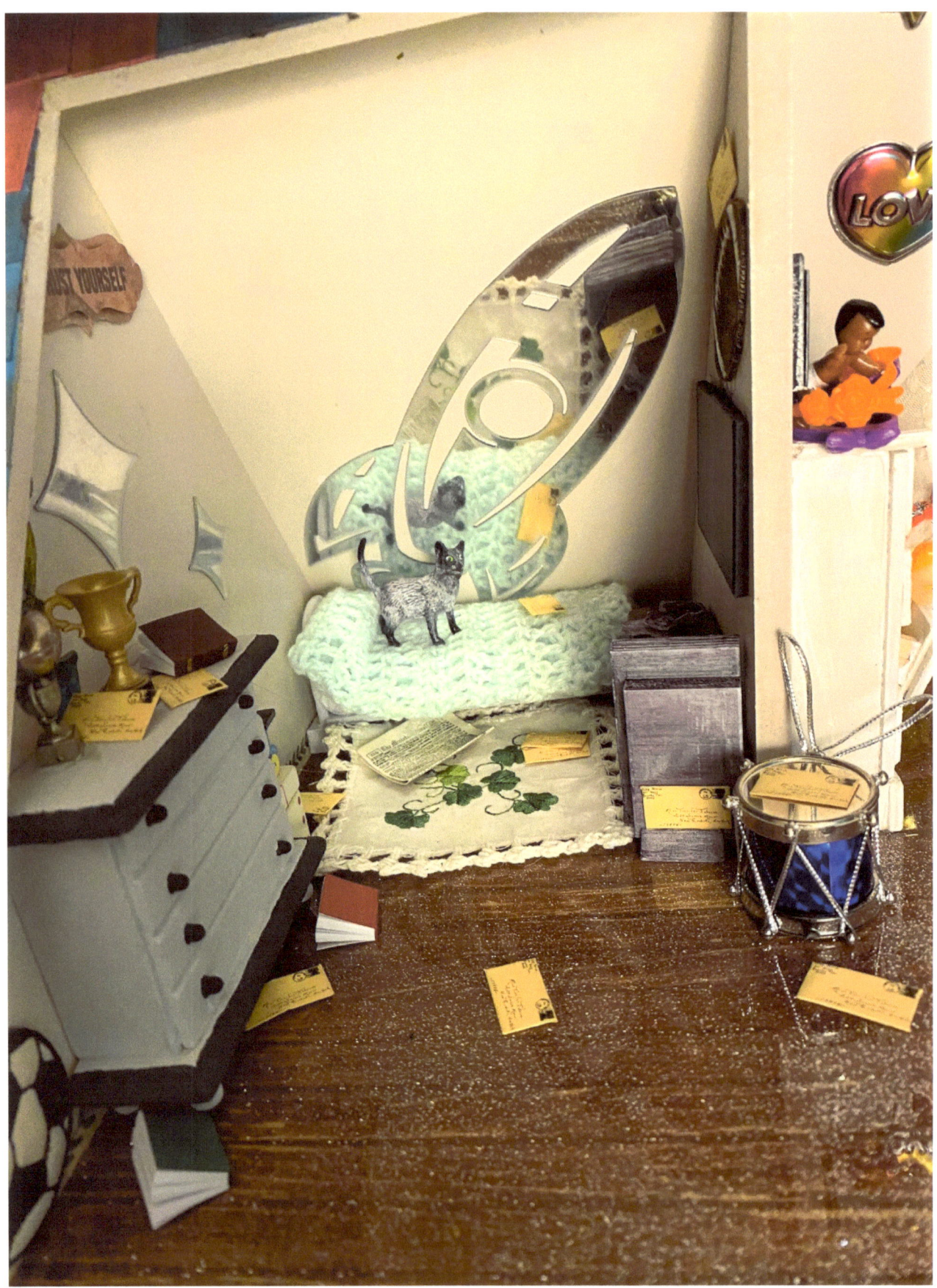

5 dollars, 3 baby dolls, pink rose, 9 purses, 4 sets of shoes, 4 yellow flowers, TRUE, 2 birds, 6 dogs, 4 necklaces, 2 shells, THERE, dress, 3 pinecones

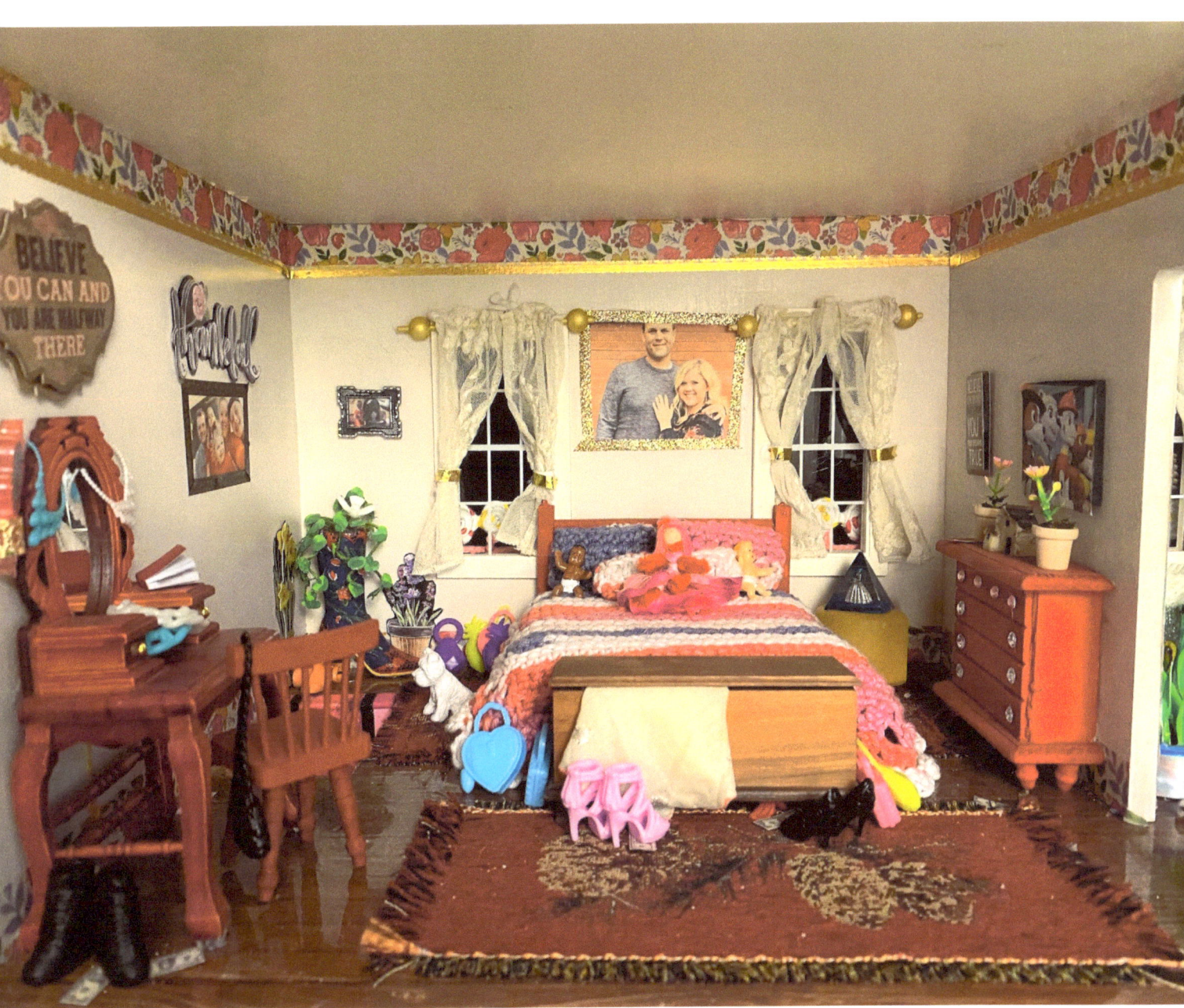

5 candy cane sticks, 1 bunny, 2 baby dolls, rainbow, squirrel, 4 large strawberries, oranges, homemade, BLESS, 6 "IT"s, 2 forks, 8 doors, foil, bakers, 2 KITCHENS

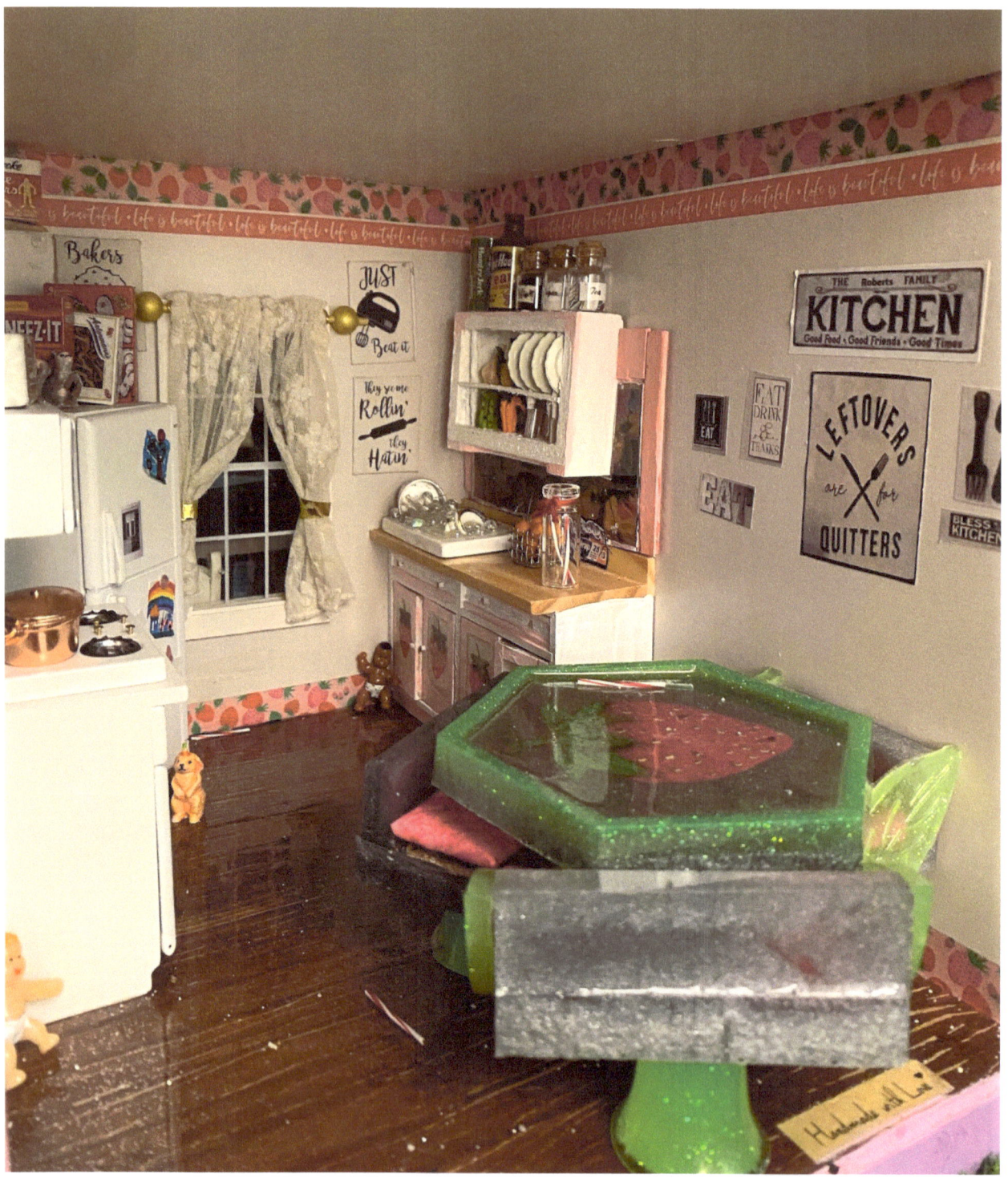

How many differences can you find from the cover?

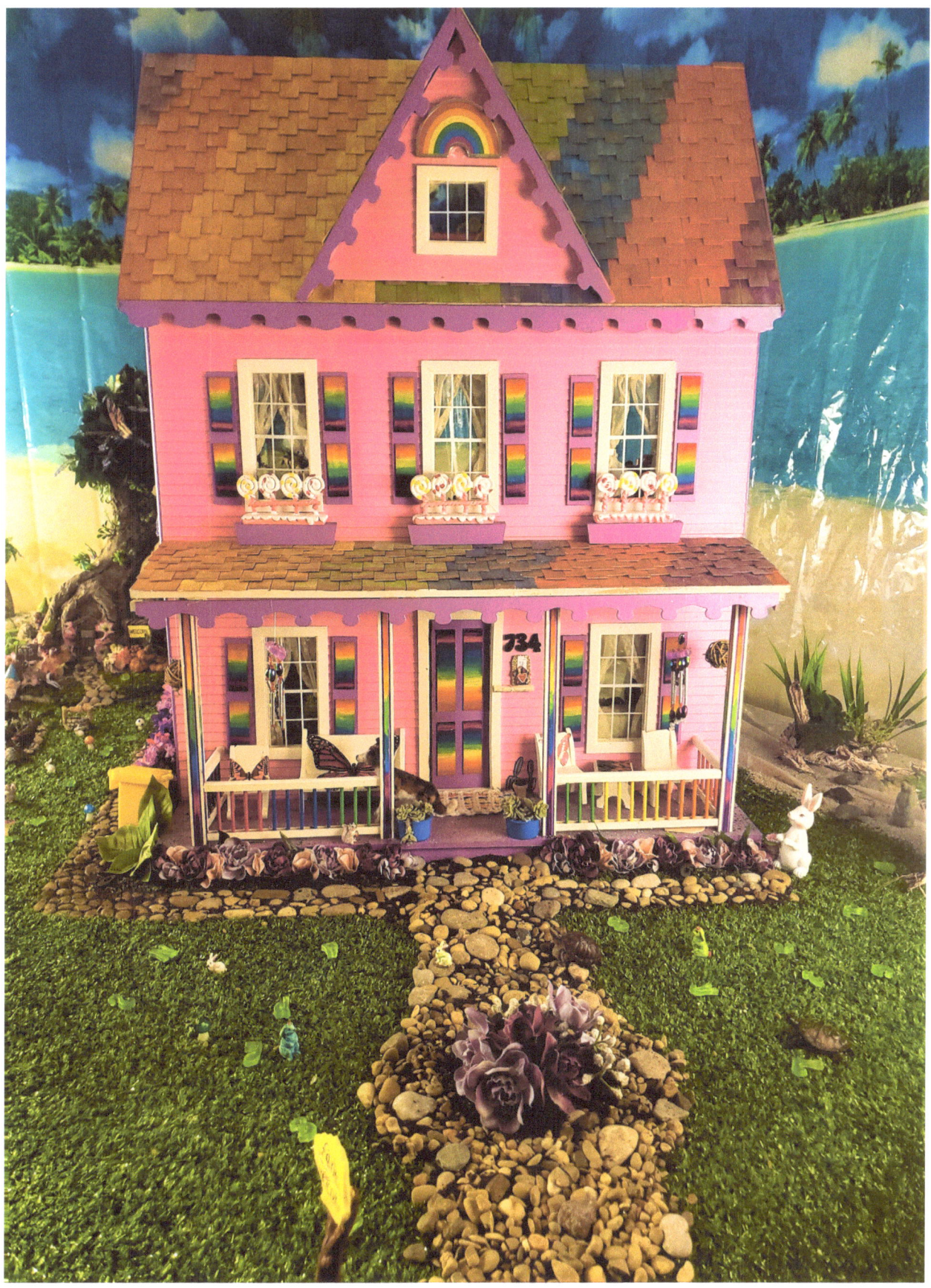

www.ingramcontent.com/pod-product-compliance
Lightning Source LLC
Chambersburg PA
CBHW040056250526
45473CB00043B/1766